HENRY
& Friends

HENRY
& Friends

The California Years 1946 - 1977

WILLIAM WEBB

CAPRA PRESS
SANTA BARBARA
1991

To Sandra Christians
who helped immeasurably in
guiding this book to completion.

Designed by Cyndi Burt.
Printed by McNaughton & Gunn, Saline, Michigan.

Library of Congress Cataloging-in-Publication Data

Webb, William
Henry and friends: the California years, 1946-1977/William Webb.
p. cm.
ISBN 0-88496-343-8 (pbk.)
1. Miller, Henry, 1891-1980—Homes and haunts—
California Associates—Portraits.
2. Miller, Henry, 1891-1980—Friends and associates—Portraits.
3. Miller, Henry, 1891-1980—Portraits.
4. Authors, American—20th century—Portraits.
5. California—Biography—Portraits.
I. Title
PS3525.I5454Z87 1991
818'.5209—dc20
[B] 90-13329
CIP

Capra Press
P. O. Box 2068
Santa Barbara, California 93120

CONTENTS

Foreword

Was it eighteen or twenty years ago that I met Bill Webb? We went on a hike out of Estes Park, and Bill was clutching his silver suitcase full of heavy camera gear. Rock climbers with ice axes and crampons dangling from rucksacks passed us. We trudged, stopping often as Bill unpacked his view camera and tripod, waited for the light, made an image, repacked, then continued on. In later years we would hike in the Sierras, stopping by Ansel Adam's cottage on the valley floor of Yosemite for cocktails, or climb in the Sangres, the Cascades, or in the coastal range behind Big Sur, and on the beaches of the Olympic Peninsula, and Pfeiffer Beach, we feasted variously on crab and mussels, lamb's quarters and morels, and sipped glorious, dusty bottles of wine.

Bill has been a friend of many writers and photographers. With him I met Ansel, Brett Weston, and Laura Gilpin about whom we later made a film, and it was in those early days of my friendship with Bill that I implored him to make photography his life's work because he had the eye for it and a gracious, affable, unobtrusive manner, but his modesty prevailed.

How lucky for us that his images will now be seen. They celebrate his affection for such friends as Henry Miller and Ephraim Doner, and his rich and unspoken connection to the universe of birds, grasses, flowers, mountains, streams, trees, and seas about which he has taught me so much.

Gretel Ehrlich
May 15, 1991

Anderson Canyon headland, with Henry's cabin on the cliff edge, 1946

Introduction

In one of his books which Henry gave me, he wrote this inscription:

To Bill —
Who, like Hitchcock, is somewhere in it but invisible to the naked eye.
                                    Henry 1/20/72

Nothing I could say would more perfectly express the kind of relationship I had with Henry Miller. The inscription, of course, referred to my well hidden participation in the book, but if the 'it' is translated to mean Henry's life, the inscription would apply equally well. I was in it, somewhere, but usually invisible!

I became aware of Henry during World War II, when I was in a camp for conscientious objectors (COs) where a few of us published a small literary magazine, the *Illiterati*. Henry fit our requirements for fearless experimentalism, and we ran a small piece of his in one of the issues.

Reading Henry got my juices flowing. He was busting the same idols all around that I wanted to bust. We looked upon the world in much the same way. Then I found the under-the-counter issues of the *Tropic's* and upon reading them discovered in Henry the reincarnation of one of my long time favorites, Francois Rabelais. Extravaganzas of dirty words in metaphors that went to the gut, virtuoso writing from exalted states of consciousness, and the warm humanity of a man in love with being alive.

It seems odd, looking back, that Henry and I so rarely talked of the many things we had in common. We came together in a business relationship, not as neighbors or simply kindred souls. A great deal of what we talked about concerned matters ranging from typefaces to royalties, for I was the publisher of one of his books, *To Paint is to Love Again*. It was usually when others were present that we got beyond the business babble.

We did have our moments of closeness, however, particularly in the later years, and especially as his son Tony was being confronted with conscription to fight in Vietnam. Henry was a dedicated pacifist, but never had to deal with the realities of draft boards, nor did he consider tax refusal, nor any other practical, possible, expressions of his beliefs. He was pleased, however, that others did these things, and I think he admired me for doing a few of them.

When Tony found himself entangled in all the considerations that face a young fellow when his government decides he is expendable in some war it has concocted, Henry asked for my help. Would I counsel Tony? During this time Henry leaned heavily on me, as he felt totally incapable of giving his son any guidance.

Yet my frequent invisibility had its advantages. I could bring a camera to social occasions and work it quietly in the background with Henry remaining oblivious to the proceedings. His exuberance, the flamboyant gesturing, the attentive listening, the wistfulness and humor, fell so easily into my camera it was as if I had nothing to do at all. I couldn't miss!

During the twenty years I knew Henry, I made a large number of negatives, never with the intention of publication, but solely for my own enjoyment. As it turned out later, these photographs had value for others and I was persuaded to bring together a group them for publication. Meanwhile, from time to time individual photographs from this collection were published in various books and articles.

Since it was never my intention to make a coherent documentary out of these photographs, many people close to Henry during his California years do not appear in this series. I regret that, of course, but that's how it is. It's most unfortunate that Eve, of whom I was particularly fond, and Hoki, Henry's fifth wife, do not appear here.

First Encounters:

How I Almost Met Henry

"Everything unusual, it is said, originates at Anderson Creek."

— H.M., *Big Sur and the Oranges of Hieronmymus Bosch.*

H.M. photo by Joseph Whitnah, 1946

In 1946 my wife and I were driving south through Big Sur, an old favorite place with memories going back to my childhood. We stopped over with some friends, living cheaply and communally at Krenkle Corners, a bit north of Anderson Canyon. They had been hired to work on some remodeling of Henry's house on Partington Ridge, while Henry and Lepska were living in the old convict camp on the headland that bordered the mouth of Anderson Canyon.

The friends were mostly fellow internees from CO camps and jails only recently released. Among them was Dick Brown, in charge of the project, Banjo Marsh, Hugh O'Neil, and Kerwin Whitnah.

During the few days we spent at Krenkle Corner, Joe and Bea Whitnah, Kerwin's parents, came down from Berkeley for a visit, and Joe, an excellent photographer, wanted to meet and photograph Henry. This was arranged and Joe and I went down to Anderson Creek. As we approached we met Lepska while she was hanging diapers on the clothesline. I stayed to talk with her while Joe went on to see Henry in his precarious cabin tilting a couple of hundred feet above a pounding sea.

I chose to leave Joe alone to get his pictures, and later decided that Henry probably had enough of visitation, so we departed without my having met him.

The photograph made a short distance north on the road as we returned to Krenkle Corner shows the point where the Miller family lived, with Henry's writing shack visible near the center. In the years since it was occupied by the Millers the property has been bought and the cabin moved back from the cliff edge. In the meantime a veritable forest of cypress and pines has grown up on the point.

I did not actually encounter Henry until 1959. Late that year I had started a small publishing company, Cambria Books, working with Henry Geiger at his print shop in Alhambra. As editor of the weekly *Manas*, Geiger had carried on correspondence with Henry Miller, and proposed that Cambria Books might persuade Miller to produce a book. Geiger wrote Henry and 'introduced' us,

"To Paint is to Love Again", Big Sur, 1960

and shortly after I made a trip to Big Sur to discuss doing the book. Long enchanted with Henry Miller's paintings, I had decided the book should probably be about painting. Henry readily accepted the idea, and before long we were both at work on *To Paint is to Love Again*, Henry to write the text, and I to round up and photograph his paintings.

The back wrapper of the book was designed to show a group of photographs of Henry at work, and this series was the first I did of Henry. He was an excellent subject, so engrossed in the painting he paid no attention to my maneuvers.

Henry began his paintings seemingly without a subject in mind. He'd stir up some color, dip his brush, squeeze it out, stir some more color, squeeze some more, all accompanied with sighs, groans, chuckles. Finally, he'd swish some paint onto the paper, randomly. This gesture would seem to lead him on, and a face, a townscape, a motto would be suggested. The painting would begin to evolve, creating its own momentum, Henry simply coaxing it along. If it got balky at any point, it was ripped off the pad and consigned to the waste basket, and the process repeated. He turned out one painting after another, each quickly once it got started.

We hit it off well and I spent the better part of the day there on Partington Ridge, in what became the usual: around a table with a bottle of wine, good talk, and a lot of laughter. On this occasion Henry and I were alone; Eve was off running errands, and Tony and Valentine had moved to Pacific Palisades.

Walker Winslow at Synanon

I had met Walker Winslow before I met Henry, during the late fifties, when he was temporarily dried up and was lecturing around the country on the evils of alcohol addiction. Under the *nom de plume* of Harold Maine, he wrote *If A Man Be Mad*, perhaps the most vivid description ever written of the tragic disturbances of the soul of an alcoholic.

Walker's sobriety, however, was short-lived. One day he called me to say he needed to go to the hospital and could I please take him. I found him in a converted garage in Alhambra, surrounded by total disarray. His typewriter had toppled onto the concrete floor and Walker was swaying nearby, barely conscious. I got him into my car after fetching the suitcase he insisted we take.

As we neared Camarillo, Walker began to sober up, and by the time we'd left the San Fernando Valley he began a repeated inquiry into my possible need to stop and take a leak. Not his need, mine. At length we arrived in Thousand Oaks, then but a wide place in the road with a lion farm and a gas station. I figured a pretense here might result in a different subject for conversation, so I went through the motions. When I returned to the car Walker seemed a bit subdued. I discovered later that he had hidden a bottle in the suitcase to ease him through the trip, and was concerned that I not be witness to any inappropriate behavior.

When we arrived at the hospital Walker waited in the reception room, along with numerous others awaiting admission. I was ushered into an adjoining office to do the admission paperwork and left that morose scene. But a little later when a nurse and I returned to get Walker, he had turned the place around. Everyone was jolly and talkative and the bottle wasn't yet empty. Naturally I caught hell from the nurse.

During this period I had become acquainted with Synanon, a pioneering drug rehabilitation facility in Santa Monica, directed by a visionary one-time addict, Chuck Dietrich. Synanon became infamous a few years later when Chuck enthroned himself as panjandrum of the world of dope

Walker Winslow, H.M., Barthold Fles

Tony Miller, H.M., Jonathan Webb, Walker Winslow, Barthold Fles, Valentine Miller, Reid Kimball

fiends, and took on the paranoia native to this position. But in the early sixties Synanon was an experiment well worth watching. Walker eventually decided Synanon was for him, and was admitted.

Walker had been a close friend of the Millers in Big Sur, often relieving Henry and Lepska from the duties of caring for Tony and Valentine. When Walker had placed himself in Synanon Henry was eager to visit him there. One day we went, taking along my son Jonathan with Tony and Valentine. This proved a memorable morning as we all sat at a long table. Henry was delighted to see Walker, though not so delighted to see Barthold Fles, the literary agent who was also visiting Walker. The conversation became animated. Henry got off a few cracks about Fles being a fraud, part of the publishing establishment that was by definition money grubbing and dishonest. Reid Kimball, Chuck Dietrich's second in command, explained how Synanon worked and Henry was fascinated to learn that literature played an important role in the therapy at Synanon. Henry seized the opportunity to offer all sorts of suggestions about writings that might be useful, for one reason or another. Quotes from Henry's favorites were brought out for comment, how they might work in the Synanon environment, and so forth. Very lively stuff!

With Henry in such superb form I began making exposures, moving around the table, and by the end of the morning had acquired a set of photos that were astounding for the variety of expressions they revealed.

H.M. in conversation at Synanon, 1962

Ephraim Doner, Famous for his Obscurity

Whether it was Ephraim's intention to remain obscure is anyone's guess, for there are abundant reasons why he should not be, and only his own reason why he chose to be. All that can really be said is that he deliberately avoided taking any of the steps that might have led out of obscurity. For Ephraim is a man of extraordinary accomplishment, passion, and wisdom. And is a superb cook, the talent of which he is probably most proud.

Perhaps it was his brief association with Chaim Soutine in Cros de Cagnes that led him to think, like Soutine, that his paintings weren't worth much, but were better than any others. However it was, only a few select souls have ever seen these paintings, and certainly no gallery owner ever has. So there the paintings lie, piled in a corner in daughter Natasha's former bedroom, awaiting the time when their custodian can no longer decline to show them. They will remind one of Soutine, surely, with their impetuous brushwork, and the heavy impasto, but, quite unlike the tortured Soutines, they are mostly jolly treatments of their subjects, often in the Hasidic spirit of dance, song, celebration.

While the paintings languished Doner made something of a living decorating ceramic tiles. Some of the spirit of the paintings spills over into these tiles, but because of the nature of the medium, and Doner's less than proficient technical ability with the chemistry of glazes and the firing, each batch of tiles came from the kiln as something of a surprise. You never could tell how they'd come out.

The glazes, often crazed, sometimes flowing over the lines of the drawings, underglazes leaking through, and sometimes only a hint surviving of what the drawing had intended, gave a feeling that you were looking at some archeological relic hauled from an ancient grave, tarnished by the ages. They are prized by all lucky enough to own one or more.

Our first meeting was over the Ping-Pong table, and I was clobbered. I later learned that Ephraim clobbered everybody, even those Chinese experts who were completed befuddled by the roars of

Carmel, 1967

H.M. portrait, oil, by Doner

the Lion of Judah, self-proclaimed at the height of the frenzy, doing his Hasidic dance at his end of the table, smashing the ball with uncanny aim directly at a well charted ridge in the table that deflected it to no-man's land somewhere in the bushes.

Doner owed his legendary Ping-Pong skills to Henry's tutoring, this being a shared indulgence in those days when Henry would stop *chez* Doner on the way back from town to Big Sur. Ephraim quickly showed a knack for the game, and before long was beating Henry in 'love' games, until finally no one could beat him.

Doner and Henry met in Paris. The story of this meeting may be apocryphal: Henry, down and out, bedraggled, standing in line at a Paris pissoir is noticed by Doner, passing by. Is he American, Doner asks. Yes. He looks hungry. Is he? Yes. Come along, then. (No one remembers whether Doner cooked up something or not. Just that Henry got fed.)

They met again some years later in New York. Doner and Abraham Rattner had become friends, and with Rattner, Henry was cruising America to catalog its failures. They were accumulating a bonanza of data in New York when they happened to run across Doner. The affinity was immediate, but the geography was against much developing. Not until the mid fifties, when Ephraim moved to Carmel Highlands, did he and Henry meet again, and this time their friendship flourished through the rest of Henry's years.

By this time Doner was solidly married to his beloved Rosa and their daughter, Natasha, had become the bright kid that so enchanted Henry. Rosa got a job with the Carmel School District as headperson of the Bay School, a venerable institution for pre-schoolers located on the shore of Carmel Bay, near Point Lobos. Rosa had a special way with kids, and soon it seemed that everybody who is anybody on the Monterey Peninsula had gone to "Rosa's School" when they were tykes.

Don (as Ephraim came to be known in the neighborhood) and Rosa soon became the most

Carmel, 1967

"The blaze of gaiety kindles in the mind vivid, bright flashes beyond our natural capacity, and some of the lustiest, if not the most extravagant, enthusiasms."

— Montaigne, *Essays III*, trans. Donald M. Frame

H.M. pastel painting by Doner

prominent and constructive citizens this privileged community had ever known.

Carmel Highlands, where my wife and I lived for ten years, is remarkable for the diversity of its citizens. It is more than tolerance that holds it all together, allows it to work effectively for community goals, maintains the lively intellectual atmosphere, and nurtures the warmest friendships of neighbor to neighbor. Parties in Carmel Highlands are amazing affairs. Not only the neighbors will show up, but sedate, conservative outsiders as well, even the high rent types from Pebble Beach will be mingling quite pleasantly with flamboyant neo-hippies from the Big Sur woods.

After much wondering about this I have concluded that the adhesive which holds all this together is none other than Ephraim and Rosa, whose attendance at all social functions in the Highlands was *de rigeur*. Ephraim could always be counted upon to put on a performance at these gatherings. He knows everyone, remembers names of acquaintances met only once, and something also of their life histories, and trots out all this miscellany, weaving a complex tapestry of all the gallants and the ladies assembled, and by the time he's done with all the toasting, the jousting, the singing, dancing and wisecracking, there isn't an awkward or uncomfortable soul in the house.

A character like Ephraim inevitably is surrounded with an aura of apocrypha. Among this is the notion that once every year Doner reads, cover to cover, *Don Quixote* and Dostoyevski's *The Possessed*. If these are indeed favorite reading matter, so is the Bible. The Book of Job and the Koheleth (*Ecclesiastes*) are obvious favorites. While he proclaims himself a "born-again" atheist, few would doubt that he is carrying on a continuous dialog with God, whether God knows it or not.

I would like to have been around when Henry and Doner really got wound up in discussion together. I can easily imagine such an encounter. Extravaganzas of words and ideas flying aloft, arms and hands following, brilliant, adventurous,

Rosa Doner, Carmel, 1967

"When he saw me, he invited me to drink with him very courteously; and I being willing to be entreated, we tippled and chopined together most theologically."

— Rabelais, *Gargantua and Pantagruel*

Big Sur, oil painting by Doner

funny, revealing. Unlike so many conversations I'd been around with Henry where he held forth 80% of the time here, with Doner, was a meeting of equals in cultivation and histrionics. It must have been wondrous.

I know from my own experience Doner's persuasive power, his ability to cut through the whipped cream. One day, as we were talking dismissively about art, he reached over to my hand, and began patting it, an unmistakeable signal that something profound was about to be delivered. "Bill, you know we're both frauds." It was curious timing, for could he have meant we were frauds for derogating art, or that we were part of that we were derogating? I never knew for sure until some years later, after the seeds from this conversation had taken root in me. (We were part of it.)

True to form, Doner was being helpfully devious. He was always doing this. Better to be a little mysterious, a little cryptic. It made one think. And think I did. It was really all about my being in a rut in photography. What started as a sly remark ended with my discovering a lot about myself and my work. There are a lot of people very grateful to Ephraim for just such reasons.

If he had aversion to anyone, it was to the phonies, whatever their persuasion. He'd trap the wine snobs by filling vintage bottles with ordinary jug wine and then ceremoniously pouring, toasting, sniffing, tasting as if it were really worth all this attention. He'd monitor the reactions quite carefully. Though dinner might proceed as usual, *he knew*!

Far too much a gentleman to expose all but the most flagrant phonies, he would usually end up performing one of his comedy acts, converting the phoney into an unwitting straight man. But given the real article, an all-facade type, Doner could be absolutely devastating. Once, in my presence, he discovered one of these, a Christian clergyman who leaked some anti-semitism. Doner landed all over him with a formidable arsenal of biblical quotations, history, philosophy, in such a brilliant

Cleaning mussels, Carmel Beach, 1967

Chez Doner, 1972

SPRING SONG

Dream back through driftwood to the nested trees,
Through bird bones to the greenshade song.
All dust is Lazarus, and the dead and gone
Split earth like flowers and bulge the seven seas.

All shrouds are shreds, and waking funerals
Make merry dancers of the walking sighs.
The Lazarus men wink pennies from their eyes,
Unrhyme their epitaphs and plant their holes.

Red over green the mocking blood works through.
Imparted in the narratives of shells
The drowned sing down the sad and wave-rung bells,
The Lazarus sea is washing over you.

— Eric Barker

"And I returned and saw
under the sun, that the
race is not to the swift, nor
battle to the strong,
neither yet bread to the wise,
nor yet riches to men
of understanding, nor yet
favor to men of skill;
but time and chance
happeneth to them all."

— Ecclesiastes 9,11

attack that the poor guy was left whimpering.

Ephraim and Henry were both close friends of Eric Barker, a Welsh-descended poet of accomplishment, who lived in Big Sur. I knew Eric slightly, after he'd had open heart surgery, following which he lived only a few months. Eric had been a jolly soul and when he knew he was not much longer for this world had issued his instructions. He wanted his friends not to mourn for him, but to celebrate his transfiguration with a wake, plenty of song and booze. And then scatter his ashes. Ephraim was to be in charge of these doings.

On the appointed day, Ephraim found among his curios a handsome Zia Indian pot and placed Eric's ashes therein. Friends assembled at Point Lobos, around a picnic table and the celebration began. As the booze began finding the right neurons to bamboozle, someone thoughtfully suggested that perhaps Eric would like a drink. Of course Eric would like a drink, and several celebrants made contributions to the Indian pot.

Eventually, the hors d'oevres and the toastings came to an end and the time to distribute the ashes had arrived. With great solemnity the jar was turned upside down. Nothing. The ashes had turned to a gummy mud and stuck to the sides of the jar. After some banging on the jar a few soggy lumps fell onto the pine needles and were kicked about a bit, thus scattering a part of Eric. The rest of him remains to this day in the jar, back among the Doner memorabilia, to receive an occasional libation from an old friend who remembers.

Today Ephraim is no longer going to parties, or holding them. His days of being the community adhesive are behind him. He is gathering in his spiritual resources, and there are a lot to gather, in preparation for his final liberation. If asked, I think that's how he'd put it. For the community, which profoundly misses his active involvement, he remains and will always remain its most cherished citizen.

In the studio, Carmel Highlands, 1966

Ephraim Doner, who lived well,
died well on June 24, 1991.
One of his last colloquies was with my son
Jonathan, who reports the following conversation:

Ephraim: *Jonathan, you are the only young*
             man I know who makes any sense.

Jonathan: *Shucks, Don, you must say that*
             to all the young guys you know.

Ephraim: *You bet I do. And I mean it*
             every time.

Florian Steiner

Tarzan dire semper veritas

*"I don't think one could put
up with him [Florian] for long.
I enjoyed him because it was
short—2 or 3 sessions.
He knows all that's wrong
with life, with us, all of us ,
and even with himself, but
he can't do anything about it.
It's too late. I don't think
his own life means much
to him, dearly as he loves life.
Why should it?
He'd be better off killing himself—
so would most of us if we
had the sense and the guts for
it. Cheers! Henry. "*

— Letter H.M. to W.W. 7/14/71

Florian is like a constantly erupting volcano, from which the prudent will maintain a healthy distance. Henry told me that in 1963 he thought twice about going to Italy, Florian's native land, for fear of encountering him. Then, when travelling in the south of France and crossing through Cros de Cagnes, he asked Vincent Berge, his driver, to speed up, while he slid down in his seat to make himself invisible. Florian's mother lived in that town and Henry wasn't taking any chances that her son might be visiting. Not that Henry didn't appreciate Florian, it simply took too much out of him to be in his company.

With all his intensity, Florian is immensely engaging. His outgoing friendliness took command of situations instantly. Wherever he went, he was always "in charge." He especially loved Brazil. On a trip into the Mato Grosso, he stopped by a rural whorehouse and made a fantastic series of photographs of the ladies, concentrating on the madam, an enormous whale of a woman. The record is one, not of poverty and ugliness, but of playfulness and warmth, and with a touch of sadness. Florian obviously set the tone for the session, which is reflected in the title he gave the series of pictures, "A Day With My Mother Mato Grosso."

Florian's photographic style was to grab images as fast as he could work his battered Pentax, then selecting from these the strongest. A familiar way of working. Less familiar was his reliance upon scrounged film and paper, usually severely outdated, development under primitive conditions with tired solutions, a dip or two in some brew called wash water. Blow ups were often at billboard size, and so casually exposed in the printing that no two of the same subject were ever remotely alike. But these photographs have great power, are evidence of a keenly sensitive eye, whether in his revealing portraits, frank eroticism, or joking commentaries.

On one of his more recent visits to Big Sur, Florian lost most of his life's work in negatives, a loss so devastating that he felt he would have to

H.M. and Florian Steiner, Pacific Palisades, 1971

give up photography forever. While he was fulfilling a liason with a lady he'd met, his rented car parked on the highway was invaded and his duffle bag, containing the negatives, was stolen. Various items from the bag were later found tossed out along the highway, but the negatives never reappeared. One may well ask, why did he haul his life's work around the world in a duffle bag? That was Florian; he didn't do things as others would.

I met Florian at Emil's in Big Sur, in 1962. We hit it off immediately. He had met Henry a few days earlier and already had made a number of "images" of him. When I saw these, along with some photographs he had taken of Aldous Huxley at Esalen, and some of Ezra Pound when he was confined at St. Elizabeth's, I was deeply impressed and wanted to work with him. Before long we'd set up a few sessions, and found that we made a good team, and we worked together many times after that.

Florian's work should become known, but that's not likely to happen while he is still in control of it. He desperately wants recognition, but makes it almost impossible. He is so prolific but so disorganized that to take in the scope of his work is much too difficult unless he directs the task. And that he can't do.

One time I set him up with my publisher and good friend, Dick Grossman, who then headed Grossman Publishers, a division of Viking Press. An appointment was made and I told Florian how to find the nice offices on Madison Avenue, where Dick was expecting to see some representative prints, drawn from a tidy portfolio. Professional, in other words.

Florian never travelled light, despite long experience. On this occasion he arrived at Grossman Publishers with an elevator full of his gear, all bundled into cowskins, full cow, Holstein, with the hair on the outside, grease on the inside, and tied up with ropes. As he got into the reception area he began to unpack this cargo and had it strewn all over the place by the time Grossman arrived on the scene: boxes of outdated film and packages of

photographic paper, sheaves of typescript, leather boots, badly dented Pentax cameras, socks, dirty underwear, toothpaste.

While Dick is fairly unflappable with the bizarre, at least the New York variety, I can imagine his dismay when he entered the reception area. In any event, the stuff was scraped together and hauled into Dick's office, in a procession which had to wend its way past a row of office cubicles. At each one Florian stopped to check out the inhabitant and, if female, would pause to exchange a few pleasantries. Always the gentleman, always funny and always loud, and very Italian, by the time they reached Dick's office Florian had won over the entire floor. He is incredibly engaging the first time around!

Dick tried to restore order by dragging Florian off to an early lunch, which he thought he might be able to endure for most of the rest of the day. But it was hopeless. The scene at the restaurant was one of loud laughter, pontification about uptight New York, flirting with any female that looked slightly eligible, generally disrupting the rest of the diners. Nor had it calmed down when, after a premature retreat, they got back to the office, for Florian had handed a sheaf of his pornographic cartoons to the receptionist as they were leaving for the restaurant. By now the drawings had circulated up and down the aisles and everyone was breathless from laughter. Grossman gave up, got into the spirit of things, and let it all go. After all, it was only money he was losing. But publish this guy? No way!

Florian had a role model, Tarzan, and more particularly, Johnny Weismuller. Once he insisted that we meet Johnny. I spent much time and effort trying to discover where Johnny lived, and finally did succeed. When Florian, trembling with anticipation, knocked on Tarzan's door, his hero opened it, almost falling on the stoop, sloppy drunk. Did an idol fall? Indeed not.

Another time Florian's hero worship got him in serious trouble while he was living in Kyoto, for the Japanese do not look kindly upon some European

"My Dear Lord Greystroke: We all know that Tarzan must eventually triumph over every adversity. Please don't forget that. Letter follows (full of admonitions and aphorisms). Love and concern, Fangio."

> — Postcard with picture of Johnny Weismuller as Tarzan, sent to F.S. in Asolo, Italy, by Cleo Mini, 10/19/67, concerning F's having contracted gonorrhea.

guy, in the middle of a rainstorm, up in a tree on a downtown street, giving Tarzan yells and scratching an armpit. It seems that Florian was lonely for the United States, having lived in Japan now a year or two, and while walking down the street noticed a Coke bottle in the gutter, a poignant reminder of the best of America. Water was coursing over the bottle so charmingly that Florian was overcome. In ecstasy, he climbed the tree, and.. the fellows in the white coats soon hustled him to the nuthouse, where he was confined for a year or so.

During his stay in the nuthouse he took to writing, in English, a series of daily letters to Henry, and dutifully mailed copies to me. Everyday for a year each of us received a package of pages from Florian. Upon casual inspection most of the content of these pages was a kind of gibberish, for which Henry had no patience, and I only a little. Within this matrix, however, were a few gems, and so I thought the stuff was worth preserving. Looking back on it years later I think I was not wrong. It is in grave need of editorial work, to which Florian would never surrender, as his writing was divinely inspired, so he insisted. No editor would have the stamina to persuade him to dot an "i".

Florian once studied with Saul Steinberg and learned cartooning. His drawings are wildly pornographic, terribly funny, or at worst grotesque. He knocks them out at the rate of several an hour, and one evening left me with a sheaf of them. Even my most uptight guests cannot avoid enjoyment of these when I pass them around. Even the customs agents, during a repressive period, had to let them through.

That was a crazy evening. Florian was arriving at the Los Angeles airport, from Bogota. He'd swindled Varig Airlines into free passage, including a ton or so of baggage. Some of this arrived in the customs area, as I was standing outside watching through the glass. The agents, seeing the amount, cowskins, and so forth, pushed Florian to the end of the line to let the less encumbered tourists escape first. Finally his turn came, and the cowskins were

H.M. and Florian Steiner, Pacific Palisades, 1971

"The only item that almost got me in trouble were my paintings, those three jokes of paintings of all things! The guys at customs looked at them and immediately recognized them as vulvas and so they took them to the boss and showed them all around and everybody studied them most seriously and they said I was not allowed to take them into Japan. Miyoko grinned a little embarrassed. As for myself I really felt with enormous balls, not as a photographer, but as a serious case of a painter being recognized for his true importance...too much! But as I finally said I didn't give a damn about the paintings and I was ready to send them to my mother in France right away, those guys must have felt guilty, especially as I had stressed they were made in the USA and all, so finally they handed them back to me with the recommendation not to show them to anybody."

— From a letter to W.W., 5/11/64

opened. After the agents had pawed through a huge miscellany of personal effects, accompanied by a running obligato from their owner, Florian began gesturing wildly to me, signalling that the fat folio of porno drawings was next. He seemed excessively gleeful considering the probability that he'd have the stuff confiscated, might himself be deported.

Not so! Florian jumped into the inspection with buoyant enthusiasm, eagerly picking out this or that especially outrageous drawing, laughing, slapping the agents on the back, being sure everyone got the full measure of humor, and if they didn't, offering appropriate corroborative gestures. I am sure this was something new for the customs agents. They couldn't maintain their self-importance in face of such a circus, and finally, in complete disarray, helped Florian pack his stuff back in the cowskins, and shoved it all out the door—no duty, no confiscation, no deportation.

Michiyo Watanabe, H.M., Florian Steiner, Pacific Palisades, 1971

Viva Ziva

"Maybe you'd be willing to take some photos of a friend of mine — an Israeli actress (Ziva Rodann). Would you? I'd get her over, if so, on that day. She thinks if she had some "breath-taking" photos of herself she could get them placed in a magazine and thus arouse a little attention. She's been here four years— has been in cinema, TV and on stage—but wants more work, better parts. Not hard to look at. Very vivacious. Think you'll like her (I like her too)."

— H.M. letter to W.W. 10/2/63.

Henry's life was never humdrum. He was constantly meeting new people, finding new causes to champion, getting new fixes on the universe. But the arrival on the scene of Ziva Rodann was something special. Henry's clowning rarely had a partner to ride the seesaw. But here she was, and a gorgeous female at that. Henry was in clown heaven. When I dropped by to make photographs, I found myself caught up in the somersaults.

Henry explained that Ziva had acted in some movie of questionable value, was a sabra and had been in the Israeli army, and that I was being drawn in to do some glamour shots for a model portfolio. We never got around to that. Ziva's penchant for horseplay brought us to the edge of the pool doing a cockeyed rendition of Leda and Swan.

Henry scrawled in big letters on his graffiti wall "Viva Ziva," and wrote it just above "Kill the Buddha!" I am sure the Buddha would have approved!

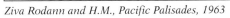
Ziva Rodann and H.M., Pacific Palisades, 1963

Elia Kazan
and
Barbara Loden

*"Those photos with Kazan and
his Barbara (and the wall!) are great.
Thanks a million."*

— H.M. postcard to W.W.4/12/67

Elia Kazan's first novel, *The Arrangement*, had just been published and it fell to me, as the publisher's representative in Southern California, to chauffeur Elia and Barbara from one celebration to another in promotion of the book. Included in this safari were visits to many of Elia's old friends and associates in the film business, but once he discovered I knew Henry he wanted to meet him above all. Henry was just as eager for this meeting, and so on a certain morning we all got together at Henry's. It was like old long-lost friends had rediscovered one another.

We spent most of the morning in Henry's study going over the inscriptions on his graffiti wall, Henry explaining each, Elia suggesting new ones, and that sort of thing. Also we took in the bathroom, papered with pictures of Henry's heros, memorabilia, poems, photographs, obscenities—a glorious mish-mash.

A gala bash was scheduled that afternoon at the home of Eva Marie Saint, where all booksellers in Southern California had been invited to meet Kazan. By noon we'd wandered off to one of Henry's favorite Italian restaurants in Beverly Hills. We were forced to keep a close eye on the clock, for I had to get Henry home and get Elia and Barbara to the reception on time. It was hardly a relaxed lunch when suddenly Henry suggested that he'd like to go to the party. I was anticipating this, for these two guys were hitting if off quite splendidly, and had a prepared negative response to the whole idea. Henry's presence at the reception would divide the attention which should be going all to Elia. It was no help that Kazan encouraged him, either. Finally we settled the issue, Henry would go on condition that he and Barbara find some obscure corner, there to hide and schmooz, until the party was over. That gave us time for dessert.

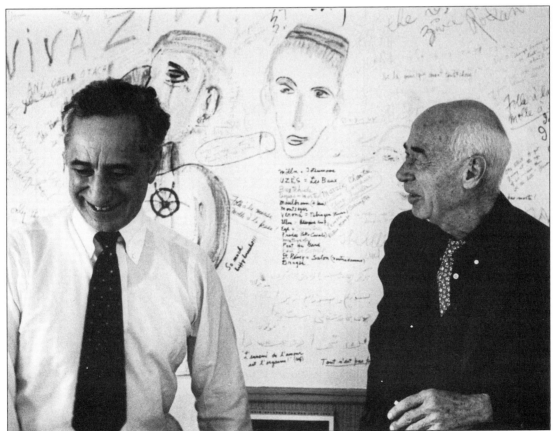

Elia Kazan and H.M., Pacific Palisades, 1967

"Just a word to say how much I enjoyed meeting Elia Kazan (and his Barbara). Wrote him (2) letters after reading the first 125 pages of his book [The Arrangement]. *It's really something! I hope it sells."*

— Letter H.M. to W.W. 3/18/67.

As it turned out Henry and Barbara did disappear for the duration of the party, and only when most of the guests had left did they emerge from wherever they had been hiding. Fortunately two of Henry's most devoted supporters, Bob Kirsch of the *Los Angeles Times*, and Louis Epstein, grand patriarch of the Pickwick Bookshop, were still there and before long an impromptu, and more intimate, reception was underway for Henry.

Barbara Loden, H.M., Brentwood, 1967

Elia Kazan, Pacific Palisades, 1967

Robert Kirsch, Barbara Loden, H.M., Brentwood, 1967

Karasu ga u no mane shite mizu ni oboreru.

— Japanese proverb.

Henry, his Hormones and his Emilator

Henry's notoriety as cocksman and the "real" Henry that I knew weren't consistent. He got his bad boy reputation for speaking frankly where others were guarded on the subject of sex. His reputation preceded him, but after I got to know him I found his language elegant and moderate, while my own was more in need of censorship. Henry probably thought of himself as part sage, part literary stunt man. It was the stunt man in Henry that inspired Emil White's emulation.

While Henry was distressed to be thought of as a pornographer, he seems to have taken some perverse pleasure in appearing to live up to that very image. Witness his permitting his editor to hire a professional nude model to pose with him at a Ping-Pong game, all in rather questionable taste. This was an occasional mode, not the Henry of rich imagination and passionate citizenship, by nature a gentleman, a devoted family man, and conservative in demeanor.

Emil White's narrow perception of Henry's character appears to have included mostly this pretended role of sexual conquistador, the fictional Henry, the courtly, romantic sexual athlete. Emil saw the fullness of Henry's being as from the edge, not the full view.

Emil met Henry in Chicago, by which time he'd read and delighted in whatever Henry books could be found in the late 30s. At the end of a workday as a waiter at the Dill Pickle Club, as he walked down Michigan Avenue, he saw approaching a person who looked exactly like the Henry Miller he'd seen in photographs. He stopped him, "Are you by any chance Henry Miller?" Thus began the friendship of which Emil made capital for the remainder of his life.

I believe Emil was smitten with the popular press imaging of Henry, not the real, ever-exploratory, ever-questioning Henry. The real Henry is not easy to know. Everyone who encounters him discovers after awhile there is so much to the man that doesn't appear right away. Henry has lived more than one lifetime; you can't readily see the

Emil White at Esalen, 1962

"PPS. For your wife—not a word of truth in Sexus. *Made it up in my head."*

— H.M. letter to W.W. 2/26/60

whole of it, only a part or two. Emil seems to have seen that part which was easiest, the hero of sexual liberation.

Did Emil believe that Henry would respect him if he modeled his life after his own limited image of Henry? It would appear so. For whatever Emil's proclivities were before meeting Henry, his life thereafter was an emulation of Henry as outrageous cocksman, as Henry had portrayed himself in his "biographical romances." Not long after his arrival in Big Sur Emil had achieved an awesome reputation for his womanizing, a reputation he did his best to promote.

Whenever an audience was gathered in Emil's presence, it took no coaxing to get him launched into a recital of his sexual escapades. He counted them up; his first black, his first redhead, his first…

For Henry this catalog was probably amusing. And surely it was for most of Emil's friends, until its endless repetition led us into boredom.

Emil came to Big Sur to be used by Henry, and to fawn in his shadow. So Henry used him, and Emil fawned. For Henry it must have been almost as good as having a dog who'd fetch the morning paper. But the service Emil gave was both real and helpful. Henry honored it in the only way he could, anointing him, as Emil so fervently desired, a "friend of Henry Miller." It was a reasonable quid pro quo. But the "emilation" included only a limited side of Henry. If Emil's worship had included more of what Henry stood for, Emil would not have made such a mess of his later years.

When the infirmities of old age set in upon Henry, he accepted them as part of the continuing opportunity to grow, to discover still more of what life was all about. He was like Hokusai, whom he much admired, the Old Man Mad About Drawing. Hokusai thought he might actually achieve a good painting if he only he could live to ninety years. Henry gave up writing in his last years, having said in words what he had to say, but he continued to paint until the very end, eagerly, every day. Each dawn was a new beginning, a new chance at

Emil White at Esalen, 1966

Emil White, Big Sur, 1969

Emil White, Big Sur, 1972

"Ducunt volentem fata, nolentem trahunt."

"I am a stranger here myself", painting by Emil White

discovery. Every day added to his store of riches, no matter if an eye was blind, an ear deaf and his legs with little circulation.

When Emil began to notice some failures here and there, he trudged off to Switzerland where some quack had persuaded him he could get a graft of monkey glands. His virility became a constant source of worry to him, and when one nostrum didn't work, he'd try another. Old age, and its conclusion, simply terrified him.

Emil was to say in his last years that without Henry he would have amounted to nothing. After Henry had died, Emil built a whole career out of having been Henry's friend, and when no challengers were about, Henry's best friend. He donated all his worldly possessions to the Big Sur Land Trust, to be enshrined as the Henry Miller Memorial Library. An earnest endeavor, the Memorial Library was, until Emil's death, mostly a showcase for his hero worship. Emil presided over the relics, recounting the same stories endlessly to the German tourists who dropped in, heroically rising above his infirmities for a few moments should some sweet young thing appear.

Towards the end of his life he did little more than wait in fear, bitterness, disappointment, self-pity. So very unlike Henry!

It shouldn't have been that way. His closest friends kept insisting that he should stop the groveling before his image of Henry, and look to his own worth. He had much to offer that had little or nothing to do with Henry. His naif paintings were full of humor and delight, as he drew upon his own history as a radical leftist, illustrated a William Blake poem, or gave us a new way of looking at the Big Sur Coast.

But as Emil would say, he painted because Henry taught him how, and because being an artist helped him to "get" women. Soon after he started painting he had a one-man show in San Francisco, and began to be anthologized in books about naif painting. But these forays into the art world, he felt, did little to enhance his opportunities with women;

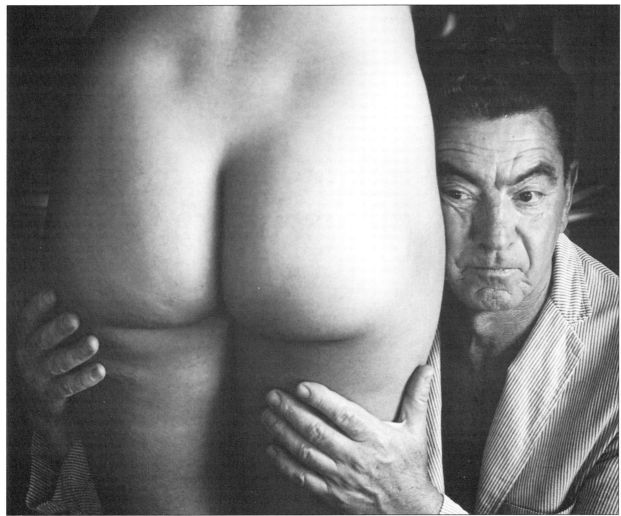

Emil and friend, Esalen, 1963

San Francisco, painting by Emil White

paintings hanging on his own walls had more clout. He tried to hoard his work rather than sell it; and when necessity moved him to a sale, he often tried later to buy back the painting.

He also had some gifts as a writer. Over the years he produced a series of guidebooks to the Big Sur, and wrote a thoughtful introduction to a small anthology of critical writing on Miller. His letters are warm and entertaining. Like Miller, he was a prodigious correspondent, though mostly to past, present, and hopefully future bedmates.

He was a storyteller too, and drew upon the rich folklore of East European *shtetls*, often decorating the tales with embroidery of his own. This occasionally brought on a scholastic debate when Ephraim Doner would challenge the authenticity or accuracy of a story, with each protagonist claiming authority for having been by Moses ordained. Often the debates were even funnier than the stories. Ephraim always seemed to have an edge when it came to the scholarship.

Henry had introduced me to Emil and we quickly became friends. At the time Emil was living at Esalen in a dilapidated cabin, after his "gallery" on the highway at Anderson Canyon had been condemned in order to widen the road and build a new bridge.

On subsequent visits to Big Sur I would stay with Emil, often photographing him and various of his girl friends. As I was making frequent trips between Southern California and Big Sur, it fell upon me to keep Henry informed of Emil's doings, and vice versa. When Henry moved to a new locale I think he consciously broke most of his ties associated with past locations. I am not aware that he communicated very much, if at all, with Emil once he settled into Pacific Palisades. Sometimes he asked if I had seen Emil recently, and if so, would inquire whether Emil's prowess with women remained still at a virtuoso level. My reply to this customary question was always in the affirmative, as was Henry's amused reaction that none, most of all himself (despite his reputation), could equal Emil.

Emil combined an impenetrable dogmatism

Emil and friend, costume by Eve Ross, Esalen, 1963

together with disarming innocence. Conversation with him, on any subject other than women, or Henry, meant dodging all sorts of hazards. It was best if one just tried to learn something, never mind offering anything. But he and I managed a mode of agreeing to disagree. In particular we'd often talk politics, the most dangerous subject of all. Emil was filled with the history of left-wing movements, had himself been an active member in Chicago of a splinter Trotskyist group. Few people understood better the workings of the state, oppression of peoples, and so on. Emil was a regular and generous donor to the ACLU, but he did not vote! He declared he was an anarchist, like Henry. But Henry would never have given a cent to the ACLU. Such confusion! We'd argue about this and other matters, never getting anywhere except back to the subject of women.

Emil's obsession had its uses for me, however. I was often in need of models for photographic projects and Emil was an agent I could always count on. He was surrounded with young women who'd be flattered to prance around in the nude for a camera, and enlisting them on my behalf gained him points.

My friendship with Emil tapered off around the mid-seventies, as he began to reveal a side of his personality for which I had no sympathy. Allowing that his infirmity was making him crotchety and demanding, that would not excuse his behavior towards his two sons. Dan and Stefan, two fine young men that I got to know fairly well, had left Australia to return to their father. That Emil proceeded then to disown them was as heartbreaking an act as I could imagine. The reasons he gave were disgusting. Dan was out because he had a lesion on his forehead (correctable) that compromised Emil's conception of what his son should be: a physical Adonis. And Stefan, an even more shocking situation, for Stefan took loving care of Emil for the last year of his life, when no one else would. Emil disinherited Stefan because he had a religion. Yet was not Emil's devotion to Henry almost a religion in itself?

Emil and H.M., Carmel Highlands, 1969

"Crazy" Lauretta

When Henry visited Big Sur in 1969 to work on the *Henry Miller Odyssey,* he made a point of including a visit to his sister Lauretta. One day we drove over to Pacific Grove where Lauretta was a resident in a rest home. Henry had been supporting her there for several years, and while living in Big Sur visited her frequently.

He had not seen her now for several years, and the reunion was touching to behold. It was difficult for either of us to have much notion of Lauretta's perception of the visit, as it seemed she was not really aware of his long absence. She simply took up wherever she thought she had left off with no apparent sense that it had been a long long time. Of course, it would have been pointless to have explained anything to her.

It was a moving experience to watch Henry's devotion to his sister, unspoken as it needed to be. Lauretta died not many years after this visit, and I believe this was the last time they were together.

H.M. and Lauretta, Pacific Grove, 1969

Life in Big Sur

Well to begin with, Big Sur is a beautiful place and anyone living, renting, or even went through it is a lucky lucky fellow. And I mean that. When it is hot it is hot and when it is cold it is cold but It has its in between momements too. It's green hills, big beautiful serene trees, It's well fed and cared for flock all caputer you with its beauty. There are places such as Nepenthe for travelers food (of course drinks too) and Deetchens for sleeping. The school is but two rooms but you learn there. There is the State Park for Entertainment too, there is the swimming pool, horesback riding, food, soft drinks, wine, ectra. Some of the great almost people who live there are: Maud Okes writer and designer, Henry Miller writer, Harrydick Ross Boss man and odds and ends man, his wife Shanagolden Ross writer, Mr. Morgan School teacher and Stable owner. These area few of the men and women who lead in helping out in Making Big Sur great. Harry Dick is a great man he helps you when you need it and who protects you loves you. Ask for these men when you come by and when you shake their hands a thrilling chill will up your spine because you shook hands of the people who started this beautiful Big Sur.

— Valentine Miller, Age 10
(pamphlet)

The Family Portrait

The brief contact I made with Lepska in 1946 was not renewed until some fifteen years later, long after she and Henry had parted company. Valentine and Tony had left Big Sur and were living with Lepska in Pacific Palisades shortly after I began working with Henry on *To Paint*.

When Florian and I paid them a visit we found Valentine hobbling around in a cast. Tony was absent, more than likely hanging out at the beach. We made a few photographs, and I think I did rather well with one of Lepska. Her loveliness and intelligence seemed to me to come together and I luckily pushed the button at the right moment.

Valentine was absorbed in being beautiful by way of fashionable hairdo, paints, and scents. I suppose that photographs of her at the time are rather rare, for not long after this occasion, when she had outgrown this teenage preoccupation, I made more photographs of her, minus the artifice. A lovely young woman, indeed.

Lepska, Pacific Palisades, 1962

Valentine and Florian Steiner, Pacific Palisades, 1962

Lepska and Valentine, Pacific Palisades, 1962

Valentine at Synanon, 1962

Geoffrey Palmer and Valentine, Big Sur, 1971

Salut, Tony!

"Happy were the ages past, while strangers to those infernal instruments of artillery, the author of which is, I firmly believe, now in hell, enjoying the rewards of his diabolical invention, that puts in the power of an infamous coward to deprive the most valiant cavalier of life; for, often in the heat of that courage and resolution that fires and animates the gallant breast, there comes a random ball, how or from whence no man can tell, shot off, perhaps by one that fled and was afraid at the flash of his own accursed machine, and, in an instant, puts an end to the schemes and existence of a man who de-served to live for ages."

— Cervantes, *Don Quixote*, Trans. Tobias Smollett.

When I first got acquainted with Tony he was polishing a surfboard in the garage, overseen by a gang of fellow surfers, all blonde, tan, monomaniacs of the waves. To talk to him of anything other than surfing was futile. And that's the way it was until conscription and the Vietnam war confronted him.

It didn't take Tony long to decide that the risk of getting killed in a stupid war wasn't his thing. He had precedents. Henry had long been an outspoken pacifist, non-political to be sure, but of strong conviction. In Henry's view there never was a war which made any sense. There were no heroes in war, only victims. To surrender one's life in a war was not an act of courage but of ignorance. Wars sacrificed the lives of many for the benefit of a privileged few. To stay out of one was the only honorable course. Henry's *Murder the Murderer* is one of the most eloquent condemnations of war ever written.

So when Tony decided he didn't want to go he had Henry's enthusiastic support. Henry wanted me to counsel Tony, as I had been through this business in World War II and presumably under-stood how to deal with draft boards and so forth (wrong!). Tony and I did talk. He would not be a pacifist in the sense that Henry or I were; he just didn't see any sense in risking his life in something so stupid as the Vietnam war. Any way that would get him out would be okay with him. Skip the principled stand, and all that. He didn't feel ade-quate to argue the pacifist position. Nervous breakdown, flee to a civilized country, drop some sugar in your pee, but to stay out of the war and stay out of jail was what Tony wanted.

My advice was to find refuge in a civilized country. But that is not what Tony did.

Some while after Tony and I talked, I was tele-phoned by Henry's secretary to the effect that Henry desperately needed to talk to me. I hurried over to Ocampo Drive and was met at the door by Henry. Upon seeing me he collapsed in tears, fell on me and together we staggered into the hallway. Tony had enlisted in the Army. It might as well have

Tony Miller, Pacific Palisades, 1971

"Can you give me name and address of your Karate friend who has a school? Tony now working as an 'extra' in films— may develop into stunt man. Wants Karate & Judo lessons. Is your friend still the best man to recommend for this?"

—H.M. letter to W.W, 6/12/67
(This friend was Bruce Tegner)

been the end of the world. There was nothing I could do, I explained, nor should we try, as it was Tony's choice and we had to assume he knew what he was doing. Tony had chosen enlistment as a last option, hoping that a higher placement in the ranks would let him escape combat duty.

Some months later I got a call from Henry that Tony had gone AWOL. Henry was much relieved, far better for Tony to be an outlaw than a corpse. He was bound for Paris, and it looked like he'd make it without a problem.

Paris wasn't for Tony, however, and soon he wound up in Montreal, which wasn't right either. Then he showed up at home. I was called in to help figure out what to do next. I phoned my attorney friend in Carmel, Francis Heisler, who defended COs in World War II and was a leading civil liberties attorney. Francis suggested that Tony turn himself in rather than wait to get caught. And he'd defend him if he turned himself in at Fort Ord, near to Carmel. The deal was made, and Tony shortly found himself in the stockade at Fort Ord. And after awhile Francis got him out, not exactly honorably, but who cared?

Life since the Vietnam war has been a deeply troubled one. Alcohol, difficulties in relationships, and so on. One might presume that being the son of a famous writer whose reputation could prove embarrassing if you found yourself in the wrong crowd would lead to "adjustment" difficulties.

Rather, Tony appears to be suffering from "guilt" about his Vietnam role. He seems to think he should have gone to Vietnam and died, or at least gone there. One of his buddies was killed in the war, and Tony seems to think it should have been him instead. His survival is only due to his "dishonorable" behavior.

Citizenship is complicated. While many knew it at the time, in retrospect we can all see that the Vietnam war was a crime against the human race. A dishonorable discharge from a criminal enterprise becomes an honorable citation of good citizenship. Salut, Tony!

H.M. and Tony at Synanon, 1962

Norman Mini

"...here we hold that not laughing, but that drinking is the distinguishing character of man. I don't say drinking, taking that word singly and absolutely in the strictest sense; no, beasts then might put in for a share; I mean drinking cool delicious wine. For you must know, my beloved, that by wine we become divine; neither can there be surer argument, or a less deceitful divination. Your academics assert the same, which the Greeks call ΟΙΝΟΣ, to be from vis, strength, virtue, and power; for 'tis in its power to fill the soul with all truth, learning, and philosophy."

— *Rabelais, Gargantua and Pantagruel*

I didn't meet Norman until after he'd left Big Sur, a disappointed novelist, and moved to Napa where he took a job as a tour guide through the Robert Mondavi Winery. Emil and I visited him from time to time, using his graces to get some wonderful wine at wonderful discounts. Even more enjoyable was sitting with him and his wife Cleo for a glorious meal and literary fun and games. Norman was a fallen away West Pointer with a vast store of literary knowledge, history, and was an expert in military strategy. He was never strategic enough to get his novel published, however.

One day we took Norman's tour. It was a wonderful piece of hokum. He was too literate for this kind of work and couldn't resist quoting passages from Li Po, Rabelais, Jesus and the rest of the pantheon of dedicated imbibers; this to the ladies in curlers and knobby-kneed gentlemen in their tourist knickers who fidgeted and tried to speed things by whispering among themselves. Undaunted, Norman would continue his lecture. Finally, in the tasting room, he would dispense samples, lecturing some more to the attentive walls and ceiling. He concluded the whole affair by dumping the dregs from bottles into a bucket which eventually found its way to his home.

For Norman was a moonshiner on the side, and from the contents of the daily buckets he distilled the most elegant *grappa* anyone is ever likely to taste. In a more earthy lecture, Norman would explain to us how he carefully monitored the heads and tails to capture the utmost of the perfume contained in these premium wines.

I've not yet had the privilege to read the great novel he wrote in Big Sur. Maybe it was never completed. He died, prematurely, a few years after we'd met.

Norman Mini, St. Helena, 1971

Jonathan Williams

The Johnny Appleseed of Letters

Jonathan continues to perform miracles of literary missionary work. Scratching and scrounging around he manages to find the bucks to bring out glamorous editions of unheard-of poets and writers. When establishment publishers were incontinent over the thought of publishing Henry, Jonathan was there with his Jargon Society, and brought out the *Red Notebook*.

Jonathan is one of those exceptional people who seems to know everyone, and is liked by everyone. He travels the world, coaxing shy literati out of their lairs, and has acquired a huge storehouse of stories, all of which he tells with exuberance and humor, for according to Jonathan, the funniest people in the world are writers. Thus Jonathan assures us that what we know to be true along the Coast is, in fact, universal.

Jonathan's occasional visits are eagerly looked forward to. We find out he's here because he always checks in first with Donor, who puts out the word. And then the rounds are made, Jonathan ever alert for some new talent, and at the same time distributing samples of his discoveries from elsewhere in the world.

Jonathan Williams, Carmel Highlands, 1965

Lawrence Ferlinghetti

Lawrence and Henry, so far as I know, barely knew one another. They shared a kind of generic address, though strict constructionsts would not include Bixby Canyon in Big Sur. Lawrence had a cabin near the mouth of Bixby Canyon, a short walk from the shore. Here he would come from time to time to write, and edit the work of others he was to publish in his City Lights Books. And here is where Jack Kerouac and Allen Ginsberg sojourned once upon a time.

While visiting at Lawrence's cabin Kerouac once decided he'd like to run down the coast and meet Henry. Lawrence made the arrangements for the next day, but at the appointed time was obliged to phone Henry that Jack had overindulged and was in no condition to make the drive.

Lawrence and Henry shared an outlook and concerns that made them sympatico, even if they weren't close friends. In his poetry Lawrence spoke out powerfully against the indifference and insensitivity of America to its artists, a theme that Henry worked again and again. To both men, Kenneth Patchen was a poignant symbol of this neglect, and both men gave of themselves to come to his aid.

In continual agony during his last years, the result of a youthful injury to his back, Patchen was reduced to penury, relieved only by occasional minute royalty payments and handouts from his loyal friends. Several of us were trying to do something for him during this trying period. Lawrence published what he could through his City Lights Books, and Henry launched public campaigns to try to marshall the faithful.

Suffering incredible pain, Kenneth was often outside of himself, lucid when drawing/writing one of his picture poems, but paranoid and very difficult otherwise, or so I thought.

In the end, it seemed hopeless that anything might be done. Whatever we were able to offer was looked upon suspiciously, as some cagey way of exploiting the Patchens, but Henry and Lawrence never gave up.

Lawrence editing Fall of America, Bixby Canyon, 1968

Lawrence at Bixby Canyon, 1968

Mary Webb, Emil White, Joanna Jarvis, Lawrence Ferlinghetti, Bixby Canyon, 1972

Lawrence, dog, Joanna Jarvis, Bixby Beach, 1972

Noel Young

A couple of mornings we went in his Jeep station wagon either for sand down at the dunes along the coast or for some rocks. There was a certain place where the rocks were reddish and a good granite rock that we could work and Henry would love to stand by and ask me how I split them and how did I chose which rock to go where, how I worked it out so that there would be no seams that would make a weak wall. He would ask a thousand questions…

— Noel Young, *Remembering Henry Miller*, 1991

Everyone who knew us both insisted it was a cosmic mistake we didn't know one another. We were roughly the same age, collected minerals, drank wine, fooled around with poetry, published books, cultivated the literati, admired Henry Miller, hung out at Big Sur, had wonderful wives, wonderful kids, loved classical music, and lived in radial houses. We were damned near twins.

Finally Gretel Ehrlich managed where the cosmos had failed. Whereupon we found additional things in common, like hot-tubbing, mushroom-induced visions of Chinese temples and dragons, birding, gardening, laughing…well, the cosmos itself.

Noel knew Henry from the early 50s, when he lived for awhile in Big Sur. When Henry needed a stone wall built at his place, an inquiry went out to Noel as to who, in exchange perhaps for a watercolor, might do it. Noel figured this was as good a time as any to learn a new trade. As it turned out, he learned quickly and well, and the watercolor is a beauty.

Capra Press, Noel's publishing company, undertook to publish most of Henry's last writing, the tributes of an old sage to his friends, most of whom had died. It was a labor of love, for Henry's last was far from his best. But they were warm recollections, a genial close to a remarkable career, and deserved the affectionate publication Noel gave them.

Noel Young, Big Sur, 1975

Yanko Varda

Varda collage, H.M. collection

Varda brought Henry down to Big Sur for the first time. I met Varda but once, on his houseboat at Sausalito. My friend Pirkle Jones was making photographs at Gate 5 and I went along one time when he told me he'd be seeing Varda. I knew Varda's work well, having once done the illustrations for a how-to book on collage in which several of his fascinating collages appeared, one of them owned by Henry.

When we arrived Varda was indisposed, laid out, you could say, on a couch in his great hollow cocoon, the listing *Vallejo*, once a ferryboat on San

Jean Varda, Pirkle Jones, Sausalito, 1970

Francisco Bay, now a derelict stuck in the mud, and home for Varda, his harem, and Alan Watts. Varda suffered from severe edema in his legs, and I could see where the phrase "on one's last legs" must have come from. Photographically it was a great day. Not only did I get some things of Varda on his couch, but many of the curios, constructions, sculptures, collages which filled the place. He died shortly after our visit, while sailing on the Bay, attended to by a bevy of sweet young things, as was his custom.

Howard Welch

Henry may sometimes have been uncomfortable with his reputation as a pornographer. But not so Howard Welch, who worked hard to create exactly that image for himself. But he was too decent a person, too warm, too clean-living, too intelligent and educated to make it convincing. Howard was at one time the "official" Big Sur Garbage Man.

I met Howard while he was deeply in the throes of building a new reputation. He'd written what he thought was the quintessential pornographic novel, something so outrageous that even the Vatican would not want to include it in its library. And Howard wanted me to represent this monument to a publisher.

I visited Howard at Krenkle Corners, startled to see he had papered every exposed piece of wall, the ceiling, the furniture, with pin-ups from *Playboy*, etc. It was a tad distracting. I tried to act blasé, pay attention to business, but this place was imposing, yet fitting, I suppose, when you're working on a reputation.

The book was a disaster. Its characters were mainly genitals without any other body parts. If there was a discernable plot, I was unable to excavate it from the tankloads of semen. As far as I was able to read, however, there was no hint of violence. And it was neatly typed. I had to tell Howard I didn't think it had much of a chance.

While he was writing, Howard was also making pornographic drawings, starting with the genitalia and ending with heads and feet if there was any room left on the paper. He promoted these as a kind of American version of *shunga*, something to tuck under the pillow of kids on their wedding nights.

Before he became a professional pornographer, Howard had driven a battered old truck up and down the ridges of Big Sur, collecting garbage from the local gentry, and in the process building a nice income from the salvage. He is reputed to have a splendid collection of discarded Henry paintings that were teased from drums of old bottles and grapefruit peels.

Howard Welch, Partington Ridge, 1977

Wynn Bullock and the Fourth Dimension

*There was the door to which
I found no key,
There was the veil through which
I might not see.*

— *Rubaiyyat* of Omar Khayyam,
Trans. Fitzgerald

*I now measure my growth as a
photographer in terms of the
degrees to which I am aware of,
have developed my sense of, and
have the skills to symbolize
visually the four-dimensional
structure of the universe.*

— Wynn Bullock, quoted in
Photographing the Nude,
by Barbara Bullock-Wilson
and Edna Bullock.

Henry enjoyed having Wynn around until he began to deliver his spiel on behalf of the Fourth Dimension. At this point Henry would despair and struggle to change the subject, without much chance of success. Wynn was a born-again evangelist for the incomprehensible. It wasn't easy to maneuver him into less esoteric realms which the rest of the human race could understand. Besides, one could never be sure that even Wynn had a very clear idea of what he was talking about.

I had admired Wynn's photography long before I met him, but got to know him when we were both included in Ansel Adams' circle, and especially after we began to work together at Friends of Photography in Carmel.

Wynn and I agreed that photography had entered a cul-de-sac. Imitation of nature had been stolen from the painters and exploited by photographers to the hilt. Photographic virtuosity was being at the right place at the right time, at which Ansel excelled. And who but a fool would try to do Ansel over again?

Wynn had an alter ego in Kazimir Malevich, whose Suprematist paintings represented struggles for liberation from representational painting into some mystical region of the soul. The Chinese painters had figured out that one millennia earlier, and I think Henry may have got it worked out, too, without knowing it. But in the West painters were generally in the thralldom of subject matter, as they had been for almost the entire history of art in the Western world. Photography was merely continuing the representational tradition. Wynn thought the Fourth Dimension, however he may have conceived of it, was the doorway out of representation and into a mystical realm. I explained to him that I understood the Fourth Dimension to be Time, and while that was mysterious, I didn't think it mystical. I thought more along the lines of the Zen archers, who by giving up thought of results, fired their arrows into the bull's-eye. Anyway, Wynn needed to get the Fourth Dimension into his photographs.

Wynn Bullock, Tina Weston, Emil White, Carmel, 1970

Wynn thought he achieved liberation by arresting large blocks of time in photographs of moving water, or by photographing nubile young women in decaying old houses. If Wynn entered bliss through these photographs I was unaware of it, and they didn't do it for me.

We agreed on one thing, that Florian Steiner was a gifted photographer, albeit of the right-time, right-place persuasion, and hardly into mystical trances. That the Friends of Photography (we called it Fiends of Photography) had declined to give him a one man show troubled us. Wynn tried more than once to get such a show hung. Florian had stored a vast collection of his work, most of it huge enlargements from his 35 mm negatives, in my basement, and it was this that we'd hoped to mount. Finally, after an internal squabble within Friends, the die-hard,

technique-is-everything, conservatives on the Board agreed to show Florian as a demonstration of their tolerance.

The gallery was jumping on opening night, when I photographed Wynn and Emil together, with the back of Tina Weston's head between them. Ansel and I strolled along together, he shaking his head, "Bill, these are wonderful images. But they are not photography." So much for what you call it.

During the 50s Wynn made several portraits of Henry, which are arguably the best ever made. Wynn had a disarming way about him, and the sitting appears to have proceded in a relaxed and jolly manner, even while one of Wynn's Leviathan Special cameras was pressed into service.

77

Henry as Nature Boy

Henry, in spite of having lived almost fifteen years in the wilds of Big Sur, remained ever the city kid. I paid a visit to the Big Sur home in the winter of 1963 to help Henry with his moving to Pacific Palisades. He made few visits to Big Sur once he'd moved south and this was one of those rare occasions, and the last one in the early sixties. The bulk of the moving was a huge stack of books, *Into the Night Life*. With a lot of help from Bob Nash and young woman visitor to Henry, we loaded my Volkswagon bus until it was sagging into the roadway, hurrying because a storm was obviously about to descend upon us.

Naturally we were a bit pooped after all this exertion, so retired into the house for a touch of wine, or whatever. Meanwhile the storm was approaching in earnest. Formidable winds shook the house, and soon rain flew by in horizontal sheets. Obviously this was no time to face the drive to Pacific Palisades down a highway notorious for landslides and washouts during even moderate storms. The four of us were marooned for the duration.

Henry became unexpectedly nervous about the whole thing, double checking the nearly bare pantry for something to save us from starvation and, more particularly, verifying that there was enough booze, given some restraint on our parts, to survive the crisis. Henry began to pour, counting each drop as if the distilleries were now in another hemisphere. I could sense that if the phone were working he'd next be calling the Red Cross.

Presently this meant a visit to the toilet. Henry was there a rather long time, it seemed, and when he returned he was much embarrassed to inform us not to get it wrong if we should need to visit the facilities and discovered evidence of prior use. Seemed the toilet wouldn't flush. I checked the water in the kitchen tap, and saw the simple truth. We eventually found a bucket, and I fetched some water outside from the fishpond, and the toilet was made functional again. All to Henry's astonishment that such things could actually be done. Still

H.M. Partington Ridge, 1963

H.M. Watercolor (1963)

the Brooklyn boy: for these emergencies you called the plumber.

Of course the electricity and the phones were out, but this was normal during storms like this, and Henry had learned to light the Aladdin lamp. We settled into tightly controlled boozing to wait things out. We didn't talk much. It was a noisy storm and we were frequently occupied having to attend to leaks, water blowing under the door, and so on. Finally, to get his mind off his impending immolation Henry thought he might make a painting, but not a sheet of watercolor paper could be found. In desperation, he tore a page from one of the copies of *Night Life* and painted over that, a constricted, fidgety little thing.

The next morning, the storm having subsided somewhat, Harrydick and Eve showed up, got up in slickers, with shovels, wrenches and other tools, ready to walk the water line and repair the problem. I volunteered to go along.

H.M., Big Sur, 1969

Harrydick and Eve

Etching and Drypoint, by Eve Ross

Partington Ridge has a community water system to which the neighborhood contributes maintenance labor. And it shows. That it works in calm weather is enough of a miracle. Held together with string, duct tape, all kinds and sizes of pipe, the water line snakes along through canyons and brush from a spring high on the mountain down to a leaky storage tank, whence it is distributed to the various houses. Because a line broke somewhere below the tank, all the water drained out, and was not being replenished from above for reason of another break. Eve took charge of finding the break below the tank, while Harrydick and I walked upward for some distance, sloshing through mud, and eventually came upon a tree which had fallen across the line and broken it. We did the repair, noting that more substantial attention would have to be given to the problem later, if ever, once one could get to town for parts.

It was a few days before I could get out of Big Sur, as the highway was blocked with a washout to the south and a landslide to the north.

Everybody on Partington, and anyone else who knew Harrydick, loved the guy. He was a particular favorite of Val and Tony. He made light of his considerable talents as a sculptor, and typically, after he and Eve became partners, encouraged her drawing and etching to the neglect of his own work. If Harrydick had a fault it was excess of conviviality, which sometimes led him to overdo his consumption of booze. The afternoon ritual with Harrydick and Eve was concerned with heavier stuff than wine, starting always with that generous Big Sur toast: "To kindness…," but all too often ending in an incoherent stupor. It was finally booze which did him in, years after Eve succumbed to the same affliction.

For a period shortly after they joined company, Eve and Harrydick were turning out one after another some very fine drypoints and etchings. I often passed along to them photographic nudes I had done, as Eve found them easier to draw from (and less expensive) than live models.

Harrydick Ross, Partington Ridge, 1976

Joe Gray

"I seek in books only to give myself pleasure by honest amusement; or if I study, I seek only the learning that treats of the knowledge of myself and instructs me in how to die well and live well."

— Montaigne, *Essays II*
(Montaigne was a special enthusiasm of Joe's)

After Henry moved to Pacific Palisades his circle of friends began to include several people who worked in the film industry. Joe was one of these. Onetime boxer, stunt man, and extra, Joe never seemed to have made it big. It is just as well; it might have spoiled him, and that would have been a great loss. Joe didn't have much formal education, but he didn't need it. He'd discovered literature years after reaching his maturity, and it had become a source of great excitement in his life. He was always ready to quote from his latest discovery, going about with his little notebook crammed with snippets of this and that. Henry actually found Joe a useful compendium of oddball information about all sort of writers.

Joe loved Henry and was a great companion at the Ocampo Drive home. I think Joe had but one love ahead of Henry: his dog, Byron. Byron, I think, spoke English fluently, probably like his namesake, for he and Joe used to have incredible conversations. I sat in a couple of times, but must admit it mostly was over my head.

Joe, Byron and I often sat together and talked around Henry's pool, watching the giggly processions in and out of the house, back and forth from the cars, of the *keisei* which surrounded Henry at the time. According to Joe, Byron had a low opinion of all this coming and going.

Joe Gray and H.M., Carmel Highlands, 1969

The Japanese Connection

When living on Partington Ridge with a view out over the ocean toward the Orient, Henry had always felt drawn to things Asian. By the time he moved to Pacific Palisades this fascination had grown into a near obsession. He read the Japanese novelists, the poets, and the Zen teachers, ate Japanese food in preference to all else, and surrounded himself with Japanese girl friends, and finally married Hoki Takuda. His friends often commented on how much Henry seemed like a reincarnated Chinese sage. To me he was more specifically like Daruma, the sainted figure that brought Buddhism to China, and perhaps travelled to Japan to bring Buddhism there also.

Daruma is reputed to have meditated for six years, and when he came down discovered that his legs had fallen off. Henry's legs didn't exactly fall off, but came close to requiring amputation, not due, however, to meditating too long, but to smoking too much. Henry's problems with his eyes also reminded me of Daruma, often portrayed with only one of them, or sometimes with eyes bulging from his head, as he had cut off his eyelids to overcome his tendency to fall asleep during meditation. Daruma was often portrayed, quite comically, consorting with courtesans. This all fits Henry quite well, especially when he'd face himself in his bathroom mirror and make clown faces at himself.

I was a bit involved during Henry's courtship of Hoki. During that period my work often took me to Henry's neighborhood and I would drop by. Sometimes we'd go to dinner at the Imperial Gardens, a Japanese restaurant on the Sunset Strip, and here he met Hoki, who sang ballads at the piano bar. Hoki knew little English, and yet sang American songs in a cute squeaky voice. She may not have understood all the words, but she pronounced them well, guided by a little notebook before her which contained all the syllables of the words in *kanji* and *kana* symbols.

We'd sit for hours at the piano bar, Henry getting all foolish in his adoration for his Japanese princess. I doubt that Hoki had much of an idea of who

Michiyo Watanabe, H.M., Partington Ridge, 1969

Henry, you goddamn son-of-a-bitch...[you] got married-wed-fresh-all-wet in za fifth honeymooney mood all legal all lawful all to be read in TIME magazine I bet, why, Henry, why? Can't you stop being an American with just one of your gals? Law-abiding anarchists, oh Christ, and you, Henry my master...

— Florian Steiner letter to H.M., April 19, 1968.

Henry was, but eventually their romance developed and they finally were married.

Hoki introduced Henry to several other young Japanese women, all of whom began to hang around his home on Ocampo Drive, some freeloading at Henry's table. Michiyo Watanabe was not freeloading, and was an appreciative companion who, with Henry and Joe Gray, took up residence in our guest rooms in Carmel Highlands during the *Odyssey* filming in 1969.

Michiyo Watanabe, Carmel Highlands, 1969

Caryl Hill

The story is fairly well known of how Henry and Eve came to a parting of the ways shortly before Henry was to depart for Europe in 1960, and how he encouraged Caryl Hill to join him there. Caryl did show up at Cannes, where Henry was a judge in the film festival, and together they visited several of Henry's European friends and publishers. And then they seem to have tired of one another and Caryl returned to Big Sur without Henry.

I met Caryl a couple of years after these events, and we became friends. She was a good model and we worked together several times, once with Florian. Caryl was of a rather languid temperament, soft and gentle, hardly "right" for the exuberant Henry.

Caryl Hill, Big Sur, 1962

Brassai

The Eye of Paris

Brassai was okay, though, it only took him ten minutes, fifteen at most, to dew up to the idea that I was no fake but an academic nut. Told him about my diploma of Uji right away, to test him, scare him a bit, too, for the fuck of it. And all the while, the more I got to like his wife—sympathies, what—the more I could feel she was getting to like me less and less... I went on about admiring those lovely torsi he's got lying all around, told him I'd already seen one of his better nude drawings in Emil's kitchen in Big Sur...

— Florian Steiner, letter to H.M. and W.W. April 19, 1968, describing his visit to Brassai in Paris

Brassai was an old crony of Henry's in his Paris days. When he visited America in 1973 I persuaded him to come to Carmel and participate in a photographic workshop at Friends of Photography. One of the enticements was that he wouldn't be far from Henry, and it followed that he went on to Pacific Palisades after his appearance at the workshop.

Brassai and his wife Gilberte stayed with us at Carmel Highlands for a couple of days during the workshop, and one morning at breakfast as we were talking in my fractured French and Gilberte's scraggly English about photography, Gilberte asked me please to take Brassai into my darkroom and show him how to develop pictures! Well, I did know that these French photographers took their processing to the drug store, but to not know *anything*? Brassai resisted, but upon Gilberte's insistence that this was his great opportunity, he allowed himself to be dragged into my lab. Of course, he paid absolutely no attention to what was going on, pleading he didn't understand English, the language in which I was performing my hands-on unspoken demonstration.

Pencil drawing by Brassai (1944)

Kerwin Whitnah

Kerwin was a jailhouse buddy of mine during WWII. After he got out of the joint he migrated to Big Sur to help with the rehabilitation of Henry's house on Partington Ridge. Like the other COs and assorted poets and peasants that worked on the place, Kerwin had his art. But it wasn't until the late 60s that he truly found his direction, a naif style full of innocence and charm.

92

Kerwin Whitnah, Brassai, Carmel Highlands, 1973

"I have always cherished old things, used things, things marked by the passage of time and human events. I think of my own self this way, as something much handled, much knocked about, as worn and polished with use and abuse. As something serviceable, perhaps I should say. More serviceable for having had so many masters, so many wretched, glorious, haphazard experiences and encounters. Which explains, perhaps, why it is that when I start to do a head it always turns into a "self-portrait." Even when it becomes a woman, even when it bears no resemblance to me at all. I know myself, my changing faces, my ineradicable Stone Age expression. It's what happened to me that interests me, not resemblances. I am a worn, used creature, an object that loves to be handled, rubbed, caressed, stuffed in a coat pocket, or left to bake in the sun. Something to be used or not used, as you like."

— H.M., *To Paint Is To Love Again.*

"I, the freest man that exists, recognize that there is always something which binds one: that liberty, independence, do not exist, and I am full of contempt for, and at the same time take pleasure in my helplessness.

"More and more I realize that I have always led the contemplative life. I am a sort of Brahmin in reverse, meditating on himself amid the hurly-burly, who with all his strength, disciplines himself and scorns existence. Or the boxer with his shadow, who, furiously, calmly, punching at emptiness, watches his form. What virtuosity, what science, what balance, the ease with which he accelerates! Later, one must learn how to take punishment with equal imperturbability. I, I know how to take punishment and with serenity I fructify and with serenity destroy myself: in short, work in the world not so much to enjoy as to make others enjoy (it's others' reflexes that give me pleasure, not my own). Only a soul full of despair can ever attain serenity and, to be in despair, you must have loved a good deal and still love the world."

— Blaise Cendrars, *Une Nuit dan la Forêt*. (A favorite of H.M.)

H.M., Pacific Palisades, 1976

William Webb
by Laura Gilpin,
Santa Fe, 1970